CLB 2231
© 1988 Colour Library Books Ltd, Godalming, Surrey, England.
All rights reserved.
Printed and bound in Hong Kong by Leefung Asco Printers Ltd.
ISBN 0 86283 642 5

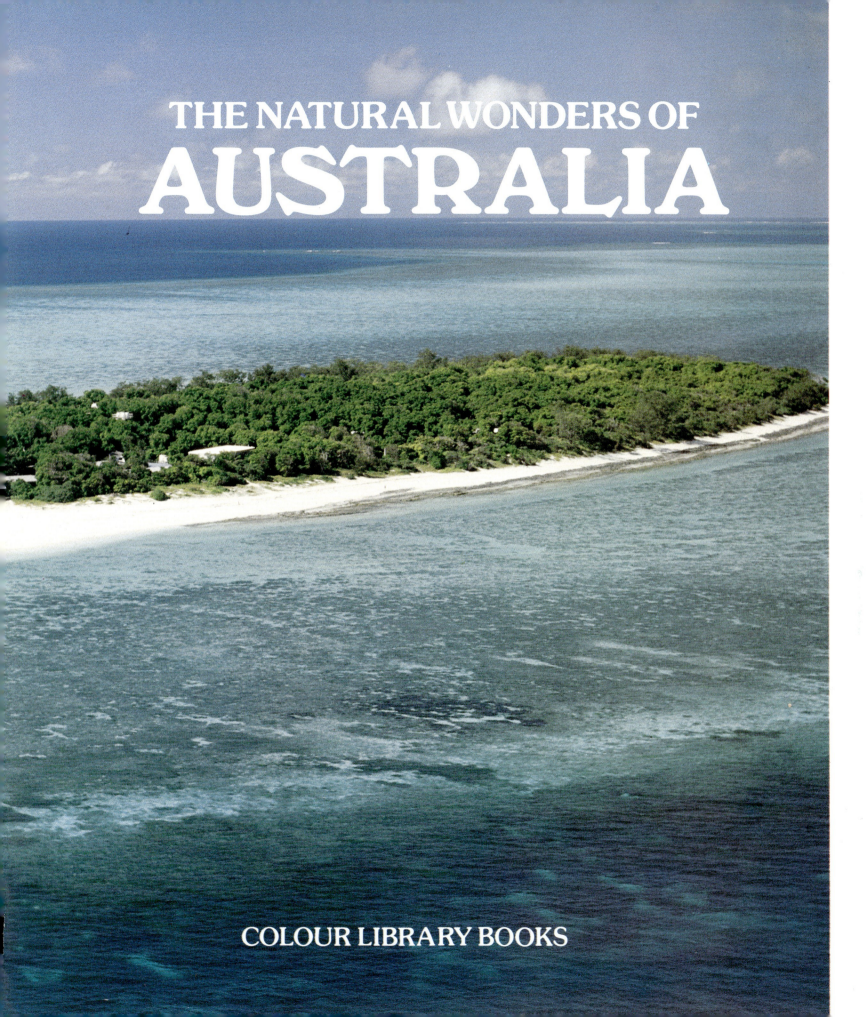

Once there was Gondwanaland.

Once, so the geographers tell us, there was a great continent which included what we now know as South America, Africa, India, Antarctica and Australia, all as one land mass. The great stresses that have done so much to alter the shape of the world about us split Australia from that great continent of Gondwanaland early in the earth's history, some 160 million years ago, isolating it from the rest of the world until the eighteenth century AD.

During that great isolation, Australian flora and fauna pursued their own evolutionary courses amidst landscapes quite unlike those found elsewhere in the world. Creatures evolved which have no parallel in other continents and survived because the competition from more advanced mammals which might have made them extinct was simply not present. Trees and plants unique to the Australian continent developed as prolific and strong species.

Despite modern influences, much of the unique quality of Australia's landscapes, wildlife and plants remains to be seen even at the end of the twentieth century, provided that you are prepared to travel long distances, often in less than ideal conditions. For Australia is distinguished by its size as much as by its unique natural environment.

Stand close to Ayers Rock, the great sacred sandstone monolith 1,143 feet high in the centre of Australia, and you would have around a thousand miles to travel in any direction to reach the sea. Australia is the world's sixth largest nation, its largest island and its smallest continent. More than twice the size of India, and four-fifths the size of Canada, Australia has two-fifths of its land mass in the tropics, yet provides three months of snow every winter amidst the Snowy Mountains of the southeast. Thousands of miles of unremittingly flat and featureless desert in the south and centre of Australia are balanced by the lush fertile hillsides, forested slopes and tumbling waterfalls of the east. The insect-ridden heat of the Northern Territory in summer is worlds apart from the crisp mountain air of Tasmania in spring.

Australia is a lifetime of experience, a mystery tour along the branch line of evolution.

Down in the thorn-bush, something stirred

More than any other creature, the kangaroo symbolises the wildlife of Australia, and yet there are fifty-six species of kangaroos and wallabies alone, and they represent only a small proportion of Australia's two hundred and fifty different species of marsupials, the ancient order of mammals which rears its young in an external pouch after giving birth to what is little more than an embryo.

The largest and commonest of the kangaroos are the Grey and the Red, which reach a height of seven feet and a weight of two hundred pounds or more and are capable of springing along on their massively developed rear legs at speeds of between fifteen and thirty miles per hour. At the other end of the scale is the rufous rat kangaroo, which is smaller than a rabbit and lives in the savannah woodlands of Australia's eastern coastal region. In between is an immense variety of species of all sizes, including one which can survive by drinking seawater. The spectacled hare wallaby, for example, which is the size of a hare, lives only on plains covered with spinifex. Prettyface wallabies stand about three and a half feet tall, and live on grassy hills. Some of the kangaroo family are found only in very small areas, like the rare, purple-necked rock wallaby, which lives only among rocks in a small part of Queensland.

Other Australian creatures were even stranger to the eyes of early explorers. The duckbill, or platypus, both lays eggs and suckles its young. The echidna also lays eggs, but looks like a porcupine. The koala climbs trees, looks like a teddy bear and can bite viciously if you try to catch it. The wombat, a nocturnal, burrowing marsupial, looks a bit like a beaver and eats plants. There is even a crocodile which lives in salt water. Other Australian reptiles include monitor lizards which have been known to grow to a length of seven feet, and the Queensland python, which can reach twenty feet. There are over a hundred and fifty different species of snakes in Australia: one to avoid is the taipan, which is among the most venomous in the world.

Even Australian birds are in many cases quite distinct. The flightless emu has, of course, become a symbol of the continent, yet there is another significant flightless bird which is exclusively Australian – the cassowary, a native of northern Queensland. Australia is very rich in species of duck, notably the shelduck and the musk duck, and there are fine birds of prey, such as the wedge-tailed eagle and the improbably-named whistling eagle. Other remarkable birds are the mound-building mallee fowl, the brush turkey, the bower birds, birds of paradise and the lyrebirds.

Mountains and Rivers of the East

The southeast and east of Australia – the states of Victoria, New South Wales and the southern part of Queensland – are among the most fertile, wooded and attractive parts of Australia. To the north and south of Sydney Heads, the entrance to the remarkably beautiful twenty-one square miles of Sydney Harbour, are twenty seven miles of dazzling white sandy beaches, and there are beaches almost on this scale all around this coast. But it is inland that the real wonders of the New South Wales terrain become apparent. The fertile lands of New South Wales and Southern Queensland are separated from the more arid territory to the west by the Great Dividing Range, a less than continuous range of hills which runs approximately north to south and bends westward at its southern end. From the Great Dividing Range flow the greatest rivers of Australia, which have made the hillsides and plains fertile and rich, as lush and green as the plains further west are yellow, brown and arid.

Due west of Sydney are the Blue Mountains, which provide some of the finest mountain scenery in Australia and earned their name from the intense cobalt-blue haze which envelops them when seen from a distance. This phenomenon is apparently due to a mist of eucalyptus oil from the trees which cover their slopes. Sheer sandstone precipices rise above richly wooded valley floors and there are many dramatic waterfalls tumbling through exciting gorges. Deep in the Blue Mountains are the Jenolan Caves, rock formations of great beauty which are some half a million years old.

Further south are the Southern Highlands, dominated by Mount Gibraltar (2,800 ft) and Mount Jellore, and, in the far south of New South Wales, the Snowy Mountains, which include Mount Kosciusko (7,316 ft). It is in this part of the Great Divide that six important rivers begin their irrigating path to the sea – the Murrumbidgee, the Murray, the Tumut, the Tooma, the Snowy and the Eucumbene.

To the north of New South Wales, in the area known as the North Coast, are some of the finest waterfalls – the Ellenborough and the Bulga Falls, both on the Bulga Plateau, spring to mind – and the mountains of the New England Tablelands. Round Mountain reaches 5,300 feet and Ben Lomond, Chandler's Peak and Capoompeta are each a little less than 5,000 feet high. West of here are the North-West Slopes, where timbered hills and fast-flowing rivers provide the natural environment for many of Australia's most important species of wildlife. The strange, volcanically-formed mountains of the Warrumbungle Range rise straight out of the flat plain around them, and the strangest of them all, known as the Breadknife, is no more than a spike of rock which rises three hundred feet from the plain and is less than five feet wide at the top. Warrumbungle National Park is a haven for Australia's unique plant life where Port Jackson figs, wattles, wild orchids and grasstrees, snow gums, kurrajongs and river oaks abound.

Further north still are the 667,000 square miles of Queensland, half of which are in the tropics, with Cape York Peninsula and the mountains of the Bellenden Ker Range, including Bartle Frere (5,287 ft), forming the northern extremity of the Great Dividing Range in tropical Australia. On the Cape York Peninsula, which has the great Gulf of Carpentaria to its west, the mountains are close to the east coast, their heavily eucalypt-wooded slopes rising some 2,000 feet only fifteen or twenty miles from the ocean, with some areas of true tropical rain forest. Here there is a great variety of rare native hardwood trees, many of which are no longer to be found in other parts of Australia – the Queensland cedar, the bunya pine, the kauri and the native Tamarind. The famous giant stinging tree has been saved from extinction, and there are some eight thousand species of plants and ferns listed as growing in the state. Two hundred miles south of the Bellenden Ker Range are the 12,000 square miles of the Atherton Tableland, wet, fertile and heavily forested, and cut by gorges full of rushing torrents. The rivers have cut startlingly deep into the great sandstone escarpments and the pools are deep and cool.

Just off the east coast of Queensland is one of the greatest natural features of Australia, the Great Barrier Reef. The world's largest coral formation, the Great Barrier Reef is also the largest structure on earth created by living creatures, and stretches southwards 1,250 miles from the Torres Strait almost to the 25th parallel. Wooded islands are bounded by crystal-clear blue lagoons, filled with brightly-coloured coral strands and myriad exotic sea creatures and plants. Giant manta rays fly through the clear water, massive moray eels live and feed on the coral floor and the most amazingly colourful clams, sea anemones and other creatures live in extraordinary, multi-hued profusion.

Beyond the Great Divide to the west the land is less fertile and becomes more arid the further west one travels. In the extreme west of Queensland are the semi-arid plains of the Great Artesian Basin, a parched, stony desert for most of the time although capable of suddenly becoming a green and grassy area when rainfall comes. West of the Divide in New South Wales is the rolling countryside of the Central West, with rich red soil, which gives way further west to the real beginning of the outback.

Australian Wildlife's Island Haven

Just off the coast is the island state of Tasmania, which was once described by an Admiralty surveyor as 'the most thoroughly mountainous island in the world'. Almost the whole of Tasmania consists of lush forests, mountains and rushing water, and the island has justifiably become known as one of the most beautiful parts of Australia. Only 190 miles by 180, approximately heart-shaped and about 125 miles from the Australian mainland, Tasmania has the highest annual rainfall in Australia. Nowhere on the island are the mountains and hills entirely out of sight.

Having been separated from the Australian mainland for between 25 and 40 million years, since the sea engulfed a land bridge to form the Bass Strait, Tasmania has a rich variety of wildlife, some of which has evolved separately from that of the mainland to produce species which are unique to the island. The mountainous terrain and the obiquitous 'horizontal', a plant which creates a virtually impenetrable thicket, make most of the southwest of Tasmania almost impossible to explore on the ground without cutting a path every inch of the way. As a result, the rare species with which Tasmania was endowed by its history have had a better chance of survival than has been the case where man had easier access.

Possibly the best known of these creatures is the Tasmanian Devil, a carnivorous marsupial which is described by some as looking like a long-tailed Scots terrier and by others as having the appearance of a small bear. Actually, it is a marsupial cat, and is black with white patches on its chest and rump. Usually about three feet long, the Tasmanian Devil is very rare, although it is reported that its numbers are at last on the increase. Rarer still, and one of the most retiring animals in the world, is the Tasmanian Tiger which, confusingly, is not a cat but a marsupial wolf. The Tasmanian Tiger is (or possibly was) striped like a tiger and of entirely nocturnal habits. There have been no firm sightings for many years, and the animal may already be extinct. Tasmania also has no less than fourteen species of birds which are unique to the island and dozens of unique plant varieties in addition to the waratahs, banksias and grevilleas which are to be seen throughout the island and elsewhere in the southern part of Australia.

The mountains of the central plateau of Tasmania rise to almost 5,000 feet and the plateau itself is almost 4,000 feet above sea level. Mount Wellington, covered with magnificent trees all year round and by snow in winter, rises 4,166 feet from the Tasmanian coastline.

A Little of Everything in the South

Along the south coast of the mainland of Australia, and inland from the coast of New South Wales and Victoria in the east and the barren coastline of South Australia in the west, one can see virtually the whole range of scenery and landscape that Australia has to offer, from rolling green hillsides, to forest, to the mountains of the Flinders Range , to open barren desert and plain.

Gippsland, in the east of Victoria, lies between the Great Dividing Range and the Bass Strait and the Tasman Sea. Flat near the sea, Gippsland has magnificent forests, and in East Gippsland, east of Wilson's promontory, a desolate headland kept as a wildlife sanctuary, there is a series of attractive and colourful interconnecting lakes stretching for almost fifty miles parallel to the famous Ninety Mile Beach on the Eastern Bass Strait.

In Northeast Victoria the Hotham Heights rise 6,000 feet above sea level and are covered with thick snow during the winter, as is Mount Buller, a 5,000 foot peak some 160 miles from the sea. The Murray River, which flows west from the Snowy Mountains in the east then turns southwards towards the sea, is the longest and greatest river of the Australian continent, and the Murray River Valley is extremely beautiful.

West of Victoria are the pasturelands of South Australia backed by one of the world's most barren wastelands, the Nullarbor Plain, where travellers are warned by signs that they will not be able to get reliable water for 770 miles. Close to the coast and the city of Adelaide is the Mount Lofty Range, where Mount Lofty reaches 2,320 feet and overlooks the beautiful Piccadilly Valley. South of Adelaide, where the Mount Lofty Range actually reaches the sea, there are attractive lakes and areas full of wildfowl – a green and wet area quite different from the dry, dusty image that so characterises South Australia. In the southeast of the state is Mount Gambier, an extinct volcano only 620 feet high, on which there are four deep and quite outstandingly beautiful lakes. One of them, known as the Blue Lake, changes colour from blue to grey each March and back to blue each November, a phenomenon for which nobody has yet offered a satisfactory explanation.

One of the most amazing sights of South Australia is the outrageous colour and shape of the craggy rocks of the Flinders Range, just over 150 miles north of Adelaide. The Flinders Range is made of immensely hard quartzites, which have resisted the erosion which flattened the surrounding plains and exhibit quite extraordinary colour. At Wilpena Pound, thirty-two miles north of Hawker, there are some amazing cliffs. Standing on purple shale, the cliffs are red at the base and white at the top. Add one of the spectacular sunsets for which this area of Australia is world renowned, and you have one of the most extraordinary mixtures of colour of which nature is capable anywhere.

The Nullarbor Plain, west of these areas of beauty, is one of the most desolate areas of this, or any, continent. Yet, despite its truly awe-inspiring emptiness, the Nullarbor Plain is no more than the southernmost margin of the great Western Plateau of Australia, which stretches from the 250-foot-high limestone cliffs which dramatise the South Australian coastline on the Great Australian Bight, across the Great Victoria Desert and more than twelve hundred miles north to the coast of the Kimberley Plateau, on the Timor Sea. The plateau is almost as wide east to west, and throughout this gigantic plain there is virtually no relief from dusty, yellow-ochre flatness until one reaches the Barkly Tableland in the Northern Territory.

The Great Deserts

Western Australia is three times the size of Texas and occupies a third of the land area of the entire continent. More than 1,500 miles long and 1,000 miles wide, much of the area is totally flat at a height of around 1,000 feet above sea level, with nothing growing except spinifex and saltbush. Yet in the southwest of Western Australia there is a fertile area with adequate rainfall and substantial forestation where there is an impressive string of limestone caves. Situated at the extreme southwest of the continent between Cape Naturaliste and Cape Leeuwin, the caves remain largely unexplored, although a few are open to the public. Those that can be visited reveal startling formations of calcite and argonite. Mount Clarence (610 ft) and Mount Melville make a pleasant change from the unending flatness of most of the rest of this part of Australia, as does Mount Barker, a few miles to the north of them.

But north of Perth and to the west are the great deserts of Australia. The Great Victoria Desert lies north of the Nullarbor Plain; north of that is the Gibson Desert. North of that again is the Great Sandy Desert, extending into the Northern Territory of Australia, where some of the greatest natural wonders of this remarkable continent are to be found. The Northern Territory is six times bigger than Great Britain, occupies about a sixth of the land area of the continent and is almost entirely tropical. In the north are the monsoonal coastal plains, which are entirely near sea level and are extensively forested with tropical trees. Between November and April, the coastal plains suffer heavy rainfall and hot, humid tropical weather that one would associate more with India than with Australia, and as a result the area around Darwin has attractive palms and mangroves as well as typically Australian trees and plants.

Further south in the Northern Territory, in the very heart of Australia, is the Macdonnell Range, which includes the awe-inspiring might of the world's greatest monolith, Ayers Rock, which measures an incredible five and a half miles around its base, and the rounded Olgas, which seem like giant reddish loaves cast upon the landscape. The Macdonnell Range is made up of heavily eroded ancient rock escarpments which have been worn to strange, unearthly shapes, and most people who have camped in the area after dark testify to the strong sense of the supernatural that the place seems to have.

But that is an enduring part of the ambience that is Australia. This is a continent which has grown alone, gone its own way, nurtured its own species and created its own natural wonders in a way that is quite unlike the natural history of any other land mass on earth. Since that break with the rest of Gondwanaland 160 million years ago, Australia has done its own thing. And there is every sign of its continuing on that course for many thousands of years to come.

Previous pages: sugar fields in the Cairns area. In the 'Winterless North', the Cairns area (above) is set against a backdrop of rugged mountains covered by tropical rainforest. The city of Cairns is famous for its natural harbour, Trinity Inlet, and big game fishing. Facing page: one of the long, white sand beaches for which Port Douglas is famous. This town, which is the closest to the Great Barrier Reef, was once the main port for the Palmer River goldfields, only to be superseded by Cairns.

Facing page: the Millaa Millaa Falls. Millaa Millaa is known as the waterfall capital of the Evelyn and Atherton Tablelands, which rise in two gigantic, scenically-magnificent steps from the coastal plains and contain jungle-fringed volcanic lakes, waterfalls and fertile farmlands. The Malanda Falls (above) are found south of the lakes district in rich dairy country, the headquarters of which is Malanda itself. Overleaf: the Fairbairn Reservoir, near Emerald, under the setting sun.

Facing page: the serpentine way of Carnarvon National Park's 32-kilometre gorge tacks through yielding sandstone in the Great Dividing Range. Blaxland, Wentworth and Lawson breached this range in 1813 to open up the outback. Above: the Moss Garden in Carnarvon National Park. Overleaf: (left) mounts Beerwah and Coonowrin, and (right) the sun setting over Noosa, the Sunshine Coast's most northerly point.

Above: a tree-studded valley northwest of Beechmont, and (facing page) Lamington National Park's Ballanjui Falls. Overleaf: (left) dense vegetation in Joalah National Park, and (right) Cedar Creek coursing through a rainforest within the Tamborine Mountain Parks.

The kangaroo (facing page) is perhaps the most famous of approximately 47 species of Australian marsupials. Above: a desert scene in the Broken Hill area, and (overleaf) Turley's Hill in White Cliffs' lunar-like opal fields, New South Wales. In places almost indistinguishable from the pale mounds of excavated earth, underground houses protect the resident mining community from the searing outback heat.

Fertile land (facing page) beside the Barrier Highway contrasts with the dustier area (above) around the artificial oasis of Broken Hill, or the 'Silver City', which provides a wealth of silver, lead, and zinc. Stored water from the Darling River (overleaf) is required to slake the thirst of Broken Hill, which lies within the 19% of New South Wales which receives less than 10" of rain a year.

Facing page: the theatrically-lit teeth of Lucas Cave, one of the famous Jenolan Caves in New South Wales which riddle the limestone of Kanangra Plateau, undermining it with caverns. Above: the plateau's sheer face juts out in stark relief against the distant, more undulent, Blue Mountains, so called because light, diffusing through droplets of eucalyptus oil exhaled by the indigenous trees, gives them an azure tinge. Overleaf: (left) a view of the Three Sisters in the scenic landscape near Echo Point, and (right) spectacular Grand Arch.

Blue Mountains National Park affords some magnificent spectacles, such as silver water from Kedumba Creek slipping through the fingers of Wentworth Falls (facing page), and the appropriately named Weeping Rock (above), whose lament holds more closely to the earth.

Above: Ellenborough Falls dropping unquiet water into the gorge below. Coffs Harbour, in the North Coast region of New South Wales, affords many superb beaches, such as Bach Beach (facing page).

The Nobbies (facing page and below) mark the extreme western tip of Phillip Island, which lies off the Mornington Peninsula, Victoria. Phillip Island is perhaps most famous among wildlife enthusiasts for its colony of fairy penguins, the 'little gentlemen in dinner suits' as they are widely known, and their nightly formal procession from the sea up to their burrows.

Above: the Nobbies, off the tip of Phillip Island, home to approximately 5,000 fur seals. Not far offshore from the Nobbies stands Pyramid Rock (facing page), a good viewing point from which to watch the colony of seals by telescope. Overleaf: young fairy penguins on Summerland Beach, Phillip Island.

Below and overleaf left: the magnificent coastal scenery of Whisky Bay in Wilsons Promontory National Park, which lies at the southernmost tip of Australia's mainland and is known informally as 'The Prom'. Overleaf right: Norman Bay, also in 'The Prom'. Facing page: richly-forested Bulga National Park, near Yarram in Victoria.

Facing page: the arid grandeur of Mount Buffalo National Park, and (above) the Kiewa River at Falls Creek. Overleaf: (left) the McKenzie River, which flows through the sandstone Grampians, cleaving mountains which rise to over 1,000m in places and affording some of the loveliest scenery in Western Victoria, such as the McKenzie River Falls (right).

Previous pages: Bridgewater Bay near Portland, Victoria. Above: one of the Twelve Apostles off Port Campbell National Park, Victoria, fashioned from limestone by constant erosion, as are the cliffs (overleaf left) of the park's coastline. Port Campbell National Park contains many such spectacles of erosion, such as the precariously-fragile looking Arch near Peterborough (overleaf right). The Island Archway (facing page) is also the work of continuous tidal onslaught.

Above: Port Campbell National Park's Island Archway, continuously sculpted through centuries by the persistent tides of a restless sea, and (facing page) one of the Twelve Apostles, standing in salt-washed isolation close to the mainland. Overleaf: the ragged shoreline near Elliston in South Australia.

The arid umber of Standley Chasm (these pages) in the West MacDonnell Ranges of the Northern Territory, is daubed red by the sun only when it reaches its noon position, from which it can plumb the narrow, walled depths and spangle with sunlight the few streams which unexpectedly relieve the land's harsh aridity. Ayers Rock (overleaf) in the heart of the Red Centre, blushes incandescently according to the position of the sun. The rock is central to the ancient Aboriginal dreamland myth in which the Red Centre is shrouded. Caves fluting its base are accordingly held to be sacred by several tribes, and bear Aboriginal paintings and carvings which depict something of central Australian Aboriginal mythology.

Above: the red earth and weathered terrain of Uluru National Park. Ayers Rock presents many faces as the soft evening light plays its infinite moods of colour across it, from sleepy amber (facing page) to an iridescent crimson (overleaf). The speedily transient phases of light and colour dressing the geological architecture of the Red Centre crown this outback vastness with the spiritual mystery recognised in Aboriginal dreamtime myth.

Facing page, above and overleaf: the rubescent, cleft domes of the Olgas mushroom in a distinctive circular grouping out of the flat desert plains north of the Musgrove Ranges and cover 11 square miles. Ernest Giles, the white explorer who first officially sighted them, in 1872, named them for Queen Olga of Spain. 'Katajuta', the Aboriginal name for them, meaning 'many heads', is perhaps more appropriate.

Top and overleaf: the interplay of light and shade accentuates the deep chasms which cleave the Olgas. Facing page: a weather-pocked slope of Ayers Rock (above). Caves at the rock's base are bitten into by Aboriginal tools to create decorations which testify to its tribal sacredness.

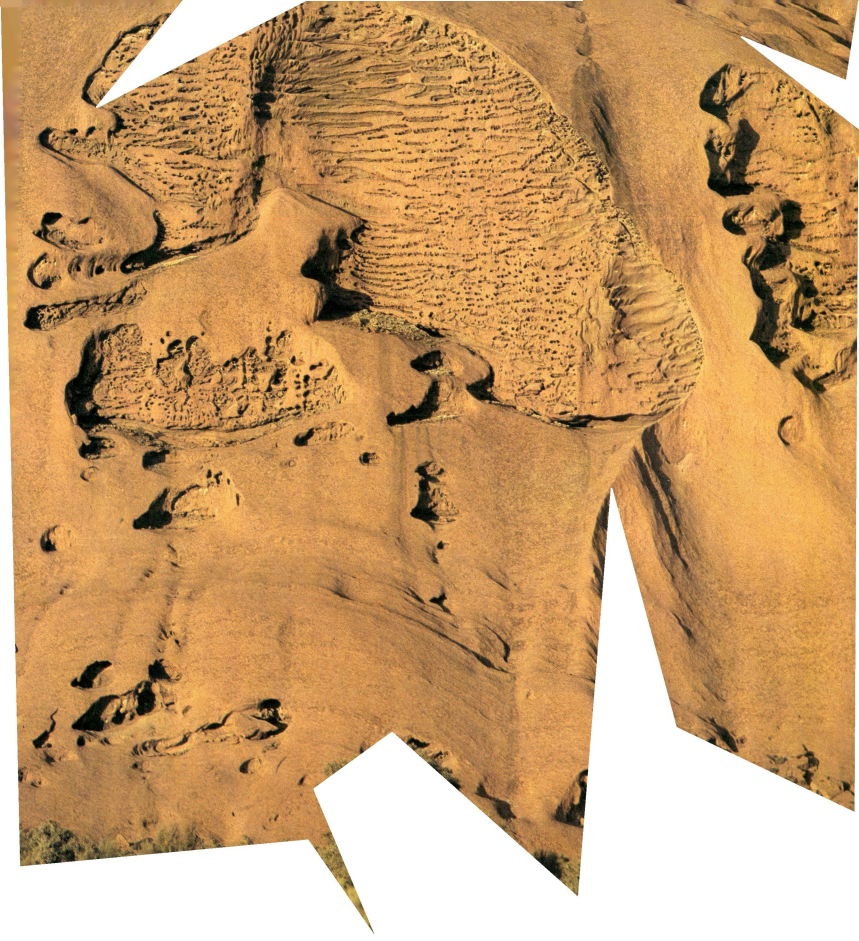

Facing page: the lengthening light of day sends shadows sliding up Ayers Rock. Ernest Giles named this rock for Sir Henry Ayers, a former premier of South Australia. This page and overleaf: the western side of Ayers Rock, where one is enabled by a chain railing to scale its ridgeline and gain a comprehensive view of the vast, baking outback, spiked with spinifex and thirsty desert shrubs, and the blue, undulating frill of far-distant mountains. This ageless rock seems curiously indifferent to the incongruous metallic impositions of man, and its sheer size, rising to 1,143 feet above the flat plain, reduces these sightseers to insignificance.

The Olgas (facing page and above) rise unheralded to a height of 1,500 feet from the parched flat plain before them, which rolls to their feet like a vast, spiny carpet. Overleaf: the variegated pink and white of the Olgas, in warm contrast to the dry khaki and olive of the tree-pricked plain.

Left: a marshland flower and (above) woodland at Fogg Dam, and (top) Berry Springs, both near Darwin in the Northern Territory. Facing page and overleaf right: East Alligator River, running through Arnhem Land and Kakadu National Park in the Northern Territory. Overleaf left: a saltwater crocodile.

Previous pages, these pages and overleaf right: the area around Fogg Dam in the Northern Territory, once central to the Territory's rice production and now a bird sanctuary. Overleaf left: a saltwater, or esturine, crocodile. These can exceed seven metres in length.

Through Ormiston National Park (facing page) deep, red gorges banking the Finke River mark its meandering onslaught on the Macdonnell Ranges. The river also runs through Glen Helen Gorge in Glen Helen Gorge National Park (top and above), and between the Krichauff and James ranges it is joined by the famous Palmer River. Right: Ellery Creek.

Above: light slides down a lake outside Darwin in the Northern Territory and picks out the spear-like trees on the shore. Facing page: pale fingers of white eucalyptus trees frame an arch for the ruddy folds of Ormiston Gorge in Ormiston Gorge and Pound National Park, at the heart of the mysterious Red Centre. The gorge is cut by a tributary of the Finke River.

Only the hardiest of plants can grow on the rugged face of the Hamersley Range (above) in Western Australia. Palm Valley Fauna and Flora Reserve (facing page and overleaf) is named for the relic palms (*Livistona mariae*) lining its waterways, remnants of a time when the whole climate of the Red Centre was wetter.

Above: Kelly's Knob Lookout, (overleaf left) a gorge in the Circular Pool, Fortescue Falls area, and (facing page and overleaf right) the candy-striped steps of the Hamersley Range, Western Australia.

The landscape of Hamersley Range National Park (facing page), which was declared an 'A' class reserve in 1969, has been eaten out of the rocks by centuries of erosion. Only hardy plants such as ghost gums and porcupine grass can live here. Below: a termite mound in the outback. Within its walled outer chambers food supplies are stored by the termites.

The anvil-shaped Loop (above) has been sawn through picturesque, maleable sandstone by the Murchison River (overleaf right) in Kalbarri National Park (overleaf left). Rainbow Valley (facing page) is a wonderworld of unlikely formations and variegated, parallel sweeps of colour compressed within the rock.

These pages and overleaf: the Pinnacles of Nambung National Park, Western Australia. In the Aboriginal dreamland scenario of the Red Centre, these almost surreal structures are the long-term results of wind, water and sand erosion shaping the desert limestone into pillars. As with all geological features of the Red Centre, their colours change according to the light.

Above: wave-beaten rocks in Torndirrup National Park and (facing page) the Jewel Caves, both in Western Australia. Overleaf: (left) Diamond Tree fire lookout, south of Manjimup, and (right) Cape Naturaliste, Western Australia. Wave Rock (following page) near Hyden, which has been undercut from granite by aeons of erosion, is estimated to be over 2,700 million years old.